ONE OF THE KEYS

A Wampanoag sits and rests close by his wetu.

ONE
OF
THE
KEYS

1676 — 1776 — 1976

THE WAMPANOAG INDIAN CONTRIBUTION

A List of Words and Definitions from the Language of the Historical Indians of Southeastern Massachusetts, Cape Cod, Martha's Vineyard, Nantucket and Rhode Island

Compiled and Written By

MILTON A. TRAVERS

Drawings By
MARIE DUPUIS

Published for the Nation By the Dartmouth, Massachusetts Bicentennial Commission

PREFACE

During this year of 1976 we proudly celebrate the 200th anniversary of the Birth of our Great Nation, The United States of America.

The year 1976 also marks the 300th anniversary of the end of the bloody King Philip's War. In August of 1676 the great patriot of the Wampanoag Indian Federation was slain on the slopes of Mount Hope at Bristol, Rhode Island. Not only does this edition bring to note a neglected but important phase of our history, it also sets in print for posterity a compilation of a portion of the lost language of the Wampanoag Indian.

The author, Milton A. Travers, has retrieved this listing of the Wampanoag dialect of the Algonquian tongue as a result of his extensive research into the history of the Wampanoags who were the Indian neighbors of the Pilgrims.

Students and residents of the area should find it an invaluable aid toward learning the story of these proud people. . . .

Indeed One of the Keys that may unlock some of the past for the future!

MILTON A. TRAVERS

Through the years, the author, who is a native of the Massachusetts area wherein the historical Wampanoags lived, has become intensely curious about the neglected history of these tribes and his research on the subject has resulted in three much needed volumes: *The Wampanoag Indian Federation,* first published in 1957 and again in 1961, *The Wampanoag Indian Tribute Tribes of Martha's Vineyard,* published in 1960 and 1962, and *The Last of the Great Wampanoag Indian Sachems,* published in 1963.

These three books and other works are the product of many years of extensive research and have gained for Mr. Travers recognition as the leading authority on the history of the Wampanoag Indians, who contributed so much to the early development of North American Culture.

Mr. Travers is a member of numerous historical organizations including life memberships in The Old Dartmouth Historical Society, Dukes County Historical Society, The Gay Head Museum Associates and the Honorary Advisory Restoration Committee of the Old Indian Church of Mashpee, Massachusetts. A retired businessman and substitute school teacher in the Dartmouth area, Mr. Travers is now a resident of South Dartmouth, Massachusetts.

CONTENTS

ILLUSTRATIONS

A Wampanoag hunts water fowl along the
shores of the Apponagansett River.

INTRODUCTION

Soon after their landing at Plymouth in the year 1620, our Pilgrim Fathers were befriended by Massasoit and his Wampanoag Indian Tribes. This friendly Indian Sachem and his people, through their wisdom and guidance, taught the early settlers how to hunt, fish and overcome many of the obstacles that confronted the Settlers in their newly chosen home.

The Wampanoag Indians owned and hunted all the lands of the Islands of Nantucket and Martha's Vineyard, the mainland from Narragansett Bay and the Providence River, including all of Cape Cod and northerly to the Blue Hills. Although this greater part of Southeastern Massachusetts and Rhode Island was owned and occupied by the Wampanoag Indian Federation, the Pilgrims and other settlers were allowed to settle within this territory with relatively little trouble. In fact, Massasoit and his thirty or more Tribute Tribes entered into a Treaty of Amity with the English that lasted for forty years until the death of the Indian leader in 1661.

Despite the fact that Massasoit's two sons endeavored to continue the amicable association with their new neighbors, an inevitable breach developed between the two cultures and a feeling of animosity soon became apparent. After the untimely death of Massasoit's eldest son, Alexander, in 1662, the Sachemship of the Wampanoag Indian Federation became the hereditary responsibility of his younger brother, Philip. It was during King Philip's reign that conditions of grave anxiety arose between the Indians and the early settlers of the area that is now Southeastern Massachusetts and Rhode Island. Finally, in the year 1675, the discontent boiled over into the war that is now history and legend.

King Philip's War marked a crucial stage during the development of our Nation. . .for exactly 100 years before the birth of these United States the events of this war between aborigine and settler did play a unique and significant part in the germination and development of our present North American Culture.

King Philip's War was the first major battle between the Red Man and the White Man. It was indeed the longest encounter endured by the two cultures here on the soil that we now call the United States. The war lasted for two bloody years and terminated into one of the rare instances in the history of the world—whereby one nation of people were completely annihilated. For that was the result. In 1676 when the war ended, the Wampanoag Indian Federation ceased as a nation of people. All their leaders and most of their people had succumbed to the mightier culture. Without their leaders, the remnants of the tribes could not rally to the cause. Those who did not submit to the colonist, wandered, as refugees, to the West lands and to the North, there to be absorbed into the tribes of their Algonquian brothers who later were persuaded to side with the French in devastating the occupied English villages of that area.

Those of the Wampanoags who found themselves assimilated into the tribes of the West, no doubt played an important role of persuasion in the Indian's attitude toward the encroachment of the White Man during his migration throughout the continent.

The frightful holocaust that history records as King Philip's War, has long been remembered and the animosities kindled then, have consumed the worst of our energies for generations thereafter.

Suffice it to say, King Philip's War cost the Colonies the astronomical figure of one half million dollars. The records state that six hundred men were killed and thirteen towns were completely burned. The homes of six hundred families were ruined. That is the settlers' losses in their ledger, but the loss to the Wampanoags included their homes and their nation.

The Town of Dartmouth was at that time one of the vast properties of Plymouth Colony, encompassing the territory that now includes New Bedford, Westport, Acushnet, and Fairhaven and was one of the areas that suffered greatly during the War. Within that vast territory all was lost except one or two outlying homes and the home of John Russell, known as Russell's Garrison, where eighteen people found refuge and survived the first onslaught of the war in 1675.

Indeed, contrastingly, the White Man's blood was left intact in the Wampanoag's Pokanoket country, where it flourished and prospered over the years into the Nation of which it now is a part.

We, the descendants of those embryonic days of our Nation's birth and today's possessors of the heritage that came to us from those times can now retrospect objectively for the Clash of the Cultures was seemingly inevitable and it must be said of Philip's character that he remained true to his people, fighting to the last for what he believed was right. Indeed, his was a gallant attempt by a great leader to preserve the heritage into which he was born.

We cannot but now weigh the benevolence of Massasoit and his Wampanoag followers in the balance of what did happen. . .and genuinely feel that he, too, by his greatness and charity towards the Pilgrims and other settlers, rightly deserves a place in history along with the other founding fathers of our great United States.

Site of the Russell Garrison - 1975

Marie Dupuis
re-contructed inside structure
Russell Garrison

The Russell Garrison is located in Dartmouth, Massachusetts.

THE WAMPANOAG CALENDAR

The Months	*The Moons*
(1) January, February	Squocheekeeswush, when the sun has the strength to thaw
(2) February, March	Wapicummilcum, when ice in the river is gone
(3) March, April	Namassack Keeswuch, the time of catching fish
(4) Late April, Early May	Sequanankeeswush, when they set corn
(5) May, June	Moonesquanimock, when the women weed corn
(6) June, July	Towwakeeswosh, when they hill the corn
(7) July to late August	Matterllawawkeeswush, squash ripe, beans edible
(8) August, September	Neepunna Keeswosh, corn is edible; or Micheennee Keeswosh, everlasting flies
(9) September, October	Pohquitaqunk Keeswush, the "middle between" or Hawkswawney Taquontikeeswush, the harvest moon
(10) October, November	Pepewarr, white frost
(11) November, December	Quinne Keeswush, the long moon
(12) December, January	Papsaquoho, to about January 6; Lowatanassick, mid-winter; Paponakeeswush, winter month

Marie Dupuis

Massasoit at Plymouth

A LIST OF INDIAN NAMES

and Notes on the Wampanoag Language
(A Dialect of the Algonquian Tongue)

Today the Wampanoag Indian Language remains only in the remnants of quaint and interesting Indian names that abound in our locality. Most of them have by careless usage over the years become so mutilated and corrupted that they barely retain the original sounds or spelling. The greater majority of their meanings have been lost forever. Although this list is by no means complete, it is a humble endeavor to help preserve a portion of the true American Language which the author has gleaned and salvaged through many years of research.

In going through the list, the student must bear in mind the fact that the Wampanoag Indians had no alphabet and no written language. Contemporary English recorders were forced to render, as best they could, unfamiliar gutturals, whistling aspirates, and other vocal sounds that had no counterpart in our language. Therefore, we have found many variations in spelling of Indian names and terms occurring in the different sources and, not infrequently, in the same source. The list of Indian names and titles that will follow will contain the most popular spellings.

To the contemporary philologist, an Indian word in its final state presented a formidable aspect, and as Cotton Mather jokingly remarked, "The language must have been growing ever since the confusion of Babel". He added that students who could master Latin, Greek and Hebrew, "were utterly baffled by the Algonquian tongue".

There were a few men like Roger Williams, John Eliot, Daniel

Gookin, Thomas Mayhew and Richard Bourne who learned by daily association with the aborigines the idiomatic aspects and trends of expressions they formed to distinguish the several combinations of sounds that lent meaning to what the Indian wanted to convey. In 1643 Roger Williams published a book entitled, *A Key Into the Language of America.* The Rev. John Eliot with the aid of Indian interpreters who had a knowledge of English published the Indian Bible that was used to convert to Christianity many of the natives.

The following specimen is the Lord's Prayer, in the Massachusetts and Wampanoag language taken from Eliot's Indian Bible. The reader's attention is called to the characters resembling a figure "8" laid on its side adopted by Eliot to represent a vowel sound that was not then contained in the English language:

"N∞ shun keesukqut quittiannatanmunach k∞wesunonk. Peyaum utch kukketaff ∞tamonk, kuttenantamoonk ne∞n∞nach ohkeit neane kesukqut. Nummeetsuongash askesutkokish assamainnean yeuyey keesukok. Kah ahquoantamaiinnean nummatcheseongash, neane matchenenukqueagig nutaquontamounnong. Ahquc sagkompagunnaiiinnean en gutchhuaouganit, webe phoquokwussinnean wuth matchitut. Newutche kutahtaunn keetass ∞tamonk, kah menuhkesuonk, kah sohsumoonk mickene, Amen". . . .and translated:

"Father ours above in Heaven. Admired in highest manner by thy name. Like done thy will on earth as like in Heaven. Let us be forgiven evil doings of ours, as we would forgive wrong doers to us. Not guide us into snares, but help us to escape from evil. Thine thy powerful kingdom, thine the strength, thine the greatest glory. Always, always me wish so, Amen."

The following is taken from the works of Experience Mayhew, one of the great philologists of the Wampanoag and Narragansett dialects:

"We did strongly love one another", may be but one word in Indian, viz. 'Nummunnukkoowamonittimunnonup'; so, "They strongly loved one another" is in Indian, 'Munnehkwamontoopanek'. These indeed are long words, and well they may be considering how much is comprehended in them. However I will give you an instance of one considerably longer, viz. 'nup-pahk-nuh-to-pe-pe-nauwut-chut-chuh-quo-ka-neh-cha-ne-ch-cha-e-nin-nu-mun-nonok'. Here are 62 letters and 22 syllables, if I do not miss my count. *(SIC^m)* The English of this long word is, "Our well-skilled looking glass makers". But after the reading of as long a word you have need to be refreshed with some that are shorter. I will therefore mention some such, "Nookoosh", "I have a father", "Noosis", "I have a grandchild", "Wamontek", "Love ye one another".

In the introduction to his book, *A Key Into the Language of America,* Roger Williams had this to say, "There is a mixture of this Language North and South, from the place of my abode, about six hundred miles; yet within the two hundred miles (afore-mentioned) their Dialects doe exceedingly differ; yet not so, but (within that compasse) a man may, by this helpe converse with thousands of Natives all over the Countrey. . .".

Following his banishment in the year 1636, Roger Williams describes his life among the Wampanoags and his friendly discourses with Massasoit: "I spared no cost toward them, and in gifts to Qusamequin (Massasoit) and all his. . .tokens and presents. . .I was unmercifully driven from my chamber to a winter's flight, exposed to the miseries, poverties, necessities, wants, debts, hardships, of sea and land, in a banished condition. For one fourteen weeks, in a bitter winter season, I was sorely tossed and knew not what bread or bed did mean. . .my soul's desire was to do the natives good and to that end to learn their language (which I afterwards printed) and therefore I desired not to be troubled with English company. . . I was known to all the Wampanoags and the Narragansetts to be a public speaker at Plymouth and Salem and therefore with them held as a Sachem. I could debate with them in their own language. I had the favor and countenance of the noble soul, Mr. Winthrop, whom all Indians respected."

We now go back to the Introduction in Mr. Williams' book and we find the following sentiment which aptly describes the inspiration that involved the work to this present day list: *"A little Key may open a Box, where lies a bunch of Keyes".*

The derivations and meanings will be from the contemporary

works and writings of Mr. Roger Williams, designated by an italicized *(W)* in citations; Mr. Daniel Gookin, designated by an italicized *(G)*; Mr. Thomas Mayhew and Son, designated by an italicized *(M)* in the citations; The Rev. John Eliot, designated by italicized *(E)* in the citations; *The History of King Philip's War* by Benjamin Church, designated by an italicized *(C)* and *(D)* in the citations for the Henry Martyn Dexter edition. In other citations an italicized *(RHC)* is for Rhode Island Historical Collections; *(PCR)* for Plymouth Colonial Records; *(BHS)* for Bourne Historical Society or Richard Bourne; *(D)* for Samuel G. Drake's *Book of the Indians; (H-B)* for Local Indian History and Biography; *(OTR)* for Old Town Records; *(MR)* for Mourt's Relations; *(IHG) Indian History and Genealogy,* by Ebenezer W. Pierce; *(MHC)* Massachusetts Historical Collections; *(NONE)* for *Places and Proper Names in New England,* Salem Press 1909; *(NONE)* also for *Dictionary of American Indian Names; (S)* for *Swanton's History of the Indians of North America; (SI)* for Smithsonian Institute; *(CHR)* for Connecticut Historical Records; and *(MAS)* for Massachusetts Archaelogical Society Bulletins.

Infrequently used sources are cited within the text. For a comprehensive and factual history of the Wampanoag Indians the reader is referred to *The Wampanoag Indian Federation,* written by the compiler of this list of Indian names.

LIST OF WORDS AND DEFINITIONS

- A -

Abenake The Abenake Tribe...from the words "Wamb-naghi", or "Wompe", or "Wamb", meaning white; and as used in association with "naghi", it takes on the meaning "The white or brightness that comes with the breaking of daylight". The word "naghi" is believed to mean, "Ancestors who came from the direction of the rising sun"...and literally transcribed, the word "ABENAKE" is believed to mean "The people with the Eastland Ancestors". (*Father Raille*) (*See Wampanoag*)

Acannotus The name of one of the Indian jurors at the trial of the murders of John Sassamon. *(PCR)*

Acawmuck "To go by water" *(W)*

Accomac "Beyond the Water" *(W)*

Acoaxet (Coaxet) "The place or 'open land' near conquered territory". This was the name of one of the Tribute Tribes of the Wampanoag Federation and was located in what is now Westport, Massachusetts. *(PCR IV:65) (SI)*

Aconaqunnauog "To thread the beads of wampum" *(W)*

Acoh The name given to their deerskin cloak. *(W)*

Aucup, Aucuppawese "A cove", "A smaller cove" *(W)*

Acushnet "At the place we get to the other side". This

was the name of one of the Tribute Tribes of the Wampanoag Federation who lived and hunted the area now New Bedford and Achusnet, Massachusetts. *(PCR IV:65) (SI)*

Agawam

"Lowlands along the water". One of the Tribute Tribes of the Wampanoags who lived in the area now Rochester and Wareham, Massachusetts. *(Adv. for Unexperienced, etc., p. 27) (SI)*

Aquetnet

"By an island" *(W)*

Ahanu

"He laughs" *(W)*

Ahtuck

"Orchard"

Akesuog

"A card-like game played with rushes" *(W)*

Akkompoin

The name of Massasoit's brother. *(PCR IV: 26; V:79) (D) (PHG)*

Akomont

Chief of the Ashimuitt-Wampanoags. *(H-13) (ITR) (D)*

Algonquian

The name applied to the Indian Nation that comprised the Eastern Tribes. The Confederated Tribes of the East which included the Wampanoag Indian Federation. *(Swanton) (SI)*

Amoskeag

"Place of fish traps". The locations on the Merrimack River, now the site of Manchester, N. H. *(NONE) (E)*

Anakausu

"A laborer" *(W)*

Annawushauog, or Annaqushanchick

"Traders" *(W)*

Anaskhommin

"To plow or break up" *(W)*

Anaskunck

"A hoe" *(W)*

Anauchemineash

"Acorns" *(W)*

Anawon

Massasoit's brother-in-law and Missinege of the Wampanoag Federation. *(D. p. 200) (W)*

Anawsuck	"Shells" (as from shellfish) *(W)*
Anum	"A dog" *(W)*
Apaum, or Umpames	"The gray-bearded ones". The Wampanoag word applied to the "Whites" at Plymouth. *(W)*
Ape-hana	"Trap - traps" *(W)*
Apome	"The thigh" *(W)*
Apponagansett	"At the place of traps where the little waters enters the big waters". The name of the Tribute Tribe of the Wampanoags whose land now is the site of Dartmouth, Massachusetts. *(PCR IV:65)*
Apponaug	"A good spot (marsh land) for shell fishing". *(NONE)*
Aptucxet	"At the fish trap in the little river" *(BHS)* *(PCR)*
Aquene	"Peace" *(W)*
Aquetequesh	A warrior leader of the Wampanoags. *(PHG)* *(D)*
Aquinnah	The name applied to the tribe of Wampanoags who lived at Gay Head. *(JEFFERS)* *(UTR) (H-B)*
Asauanash	The painted plumbstones which they tossed and played as dice. *(W)*
Ashappock	"Hemp" *(W)*
Ashaunt-(Teaug)	"Lobster - (Lobsters)" *(W)*
Ashowoohanitt	Chief of the Coakashoise-Wampanoags. *(H-B)* *(UTR)*
Ashimuitt	The name of one of the Wampanoag Tribute Tribes located on Cape Cod, Massachusetts. *(H-B) (OTR) (D)*
Askug	"A snake" *(W)*

Askutasquash   The Indian squash which was about the size of an apple. *(W)*

Askwitteachick   "A sentinel" *(W)*

Aspinet   The chief of the Nausett-Wampanoags. *(PCR) (MR) (PHG)*

Assameekg   The name of one of the Wampanoag Tribute Tribes located on Cape Cod, Massachusetts. *(H-B) (OTR) (SI)*

Assasamoogh   The first Christian Indian preacher on Nantucket, Massachusetts. He was called "John Gibbs" and his favorite preaching place on the island is still called "Gibbs' Pond". *(M) (OTR) (H-B)*

Assawompsett   "The great inland water at the place of the white stones." This word is believed to have been contracted from the original sound of "HASSA-wompsett". Assawompsett Pond at Lakeville, Massachusetts is the largest inland fresh water pond in Massachusetts. This was the name given to the Wampanoag Tribute Tribe located in this area. *(WINTHROP'S JOURNAL, 11:121 NOTE) (W) (H-B) (OTR)*

Assonet   "The stone place". One of the Wampanoag Tribute Tribes located in the area now Assonet and Freetown, Massachusetts. *(OTR) (D) (H-B)*

Assonnooshque   "A giver of victuals". The name of an Indian known as "Old Sarah" of Edgartown, Massachusetts. *(H-B) (OTR)*

Assowetough   A daughter of the Indian, John Sassamon. *(PHE) (PCR XII 229, 230, 235)*

Atauskawaw-Wauog   "Wampanoag Indian Princes (Lords)". The name given to male heirs to Sachemships. *(W)*

Attitaash   "Blue berries or huckle berries" *(W)*

Attuck, Quock or   "Deer" *(W)*
  Noonatch
  Noonat-Chaug

Audta	"A pair of small breeches or apron" *(W)*
Auke or Sanaukamuck	"Ground or land" *(W)*
Auke Taquatsha	"The ground is frozen" *(W)*
Aukeeteahettit	"Time to prepare earth for planting" *(W)*
Aukeeteaumitch	"Planting time" *(W)*
Aumanep	"Fishing line" *(W)*
Aumansk Waukanunosint	"A fort" *(W)*
Aumsuog or Munnawhatteaug	"The herring fish (alewives)" *(W)*
Aunan-Quuneke	"A doe" *(W)*
Aunckuck-Quauog	"Heath-fowl" — Heathen (now extinct) *(W)*
Auquannash	"Root cellars" (where they stored grain, etc.) *(W)*
Ausup-pannog	"A raccoon - raccoons" *(W)*
Autah, Autawhun or Petunk	Name given to their "pocket apron" *(W)*
Awashonks	The Squaw Sachem of the Sakonnets, a Tribute Tribe of the Wampanoags who lived in the area now Little Compton, Rhode Island. *(DRAKE-250) (MHC X 114) (PCR V:75; VI:113; VII:191)*
Awaun-nakommit	"One who makes a feast" *(W)*
Awaunagrs-suck	"Englishman-Englishmen" — actually means "the strangers". *(W)*
Awepu	"A truce" or "The peace between battles". *(W)*

- B -

Betokom, Symon	A praying Indian from Wamesit. *(E)*

- C -

Canonchet	The son of Miantonomo and last Sachem of the Narragansett Indian Federation. *(D) (RHC)*

Canonicus   A famous Sachem of the Narraganset Federation. *(D)*

Capat   "Ice" *(W)*

Capowack   "Those who harbor others (the refugee place)". The Indian name applied to the group of four Wampanoag Tribute Tribes at Martha's Vineyard. *(M) (E)*

Catachukutcho   The Gay Head (hill). Indian name for Gay Head, Martha's Vineyard, Massachusetts.

Caukoanash   "Deer skin stockings" *(W)*

Cauompsk   "A whetstone" *(W)*

Cauquat-tash   "Arrow - arrows" *(W)*

Causkashunck   "The deer skin" *(W)*

Cawnacome   The chief of the Manomet-Wampanoags of Cape Cod. *(D) (OTR)*

Chappaquiddick   "An island that stands alone next to a larger one". The name of one of the Wampanoag Tribute Tribes on Martha's Vineyard. *(NONE) (OTR)*

Chauquaquock   "Sword-men". Another Indian name for the Englishmen. *(W)*

Cheeschanmuck   The son of one of the Chiefs at Martha's Vineyard. He was a Harvard Indian College graduate in the year 1665. *(D) (M) (E)*

Chekesitch   "The northwest wind" *(W)*

Chekesu   "The northwest" *(W)*

Chepasquaw   "A dead woman" *(W)*

Chepewessin   "The northeast" *(W)*

Chepian   One of the names applied to an evil spirit. *(W)*

Chichegin   "A hatchet" *(W)*

Chicka   One of the names applied to the Chief's house. *(W)*

Chickatubut	The name of one of the Chiefs who lived in the area now Weymouth, Massachusetts. It means "A house on fire". Sachem of Massachusetts Indian Federation. *(MHC) (D)*
Chickauta-wetu	"A house that has been set on fire" *(W)*
Chippewas	A tribe of Indians native to Lake Superior. *(S)*
Chkesuwand	"The God of the Western winds" *(W)*
Chobonekonhonom	The Indian name of the area now Dudley, Massachusetts. *(MHC) (D)*
Chogan-Euck	"Black bird - black birds" *(W)*
Chowahunna	A Sakonnet Indian *(D-250) (MHC X 114)*
Coatuit	The name of the Wampanoag Tribute Tribe once located on Cape Cod, Massachusetts. *(B-H) (OTR) (SI)*
Cocheset	"A place of small pine trees" (West Bridgewater) *(W)*
Cohannet	"A long cleared place". The name of the Wampanoag Tribute Tribe native to the area that is now Taunton, Massachusetts. *(NONE) (D) (W) (SI)*
Cohasset	"Long stone place". The name of a Wampanoag Tribute Tribe once located in the Cape Cod area. *(B-H) (OTR) (SI)*
Cokashoise	Another Wampanoag Tribute Tribe native to the area now Cape Cod, Massachusetts. *(B-H) (OTR) (SI)*
Connecticut	"A very long waterway used by all the people" — from "Con" meaning long, and "Titicut" meaning "the waterway traveled by all". *(NONE) (W) (E. Gen. XV:18)*
Cooxisset	One of the Wampanoag Tribute Tribes once located on Cape Cod, Massachusetts. *(B-H) (OTR) (SI)*
Coquasqusict	A Wampanoag Tribute Tribe once located on Cape Cod, Massachusetts. *(B-H) (OTR) (SI)*

Corbitant
A Sagamore of the Wampanoag Indian Federation, and Chief of the Mattapoisett and Pocasset Tribute Tribes of the Wampanoags that were native to the territory now Swansea and Fall River, Massachusetts and Tiverton, Rhode Island. It is believed that he was the father of Weetammo. *(D) (IHG) (MR)*

Cotatamhea
"A physic drink" *(W)*

Cowaw-esuck
"Pine tree (young pine sapling)" *(W)*

Cowsumpsit
A Wampanoag Tribute Tribe once located on Cape Cod, Massachusetts. *(H-B) (OTR) (SI)*

Cowwewonck
"The soul or spirit" *(W)*

Cummaquid
The Indian name of Barnstable Harbor in Massachusetts. *(BHS) (TALES OF CAPE COD, INC.)*

Cuppi-machaug
"Thick wood (a swamp)" *(W)*

Cushnet
A mutilation of the word, Achusnet. *(PCR-IV:65)*

Cutshamakin
The chief of the tribe once native to Dorchester, Massachusetts. *(E) (MHC) (G)*

Cutshausha
"The lightning" *(W)*

Cuttyhunk
"Land lying high out of the water". The name of Cuttyhunk Island, Massachusetts. *(NONE)*

- E -

Eataubana
"Old traps" *(W)*

Enewashim
"A male animal" *(W)*

Enomphommin
"To thread or string" *(W)*

Enomphosachick or Wampumpeag
"Strung beads" with Wampumpeag being the plural word meaning "the strung wampum". *(W)*

Epanow (Apanno)
A Sagamore of the Wampanoag Indian Fed-

eration and also Sachem of the Tribute Tribes on Martha's Vineyard, Massachusetts. *(D) (PCR) (B-H)*

Etchemin "Canoe men" as applied to a Tribute Tribe of the Abenakes. *(FATHER RAILLE) (NONE)*

Etouwawayi "Wooly cloth" *(W)*

Ewachim-neash "Corn" (maize) *(W)*

- F -

Foxun A Mohegan Indian. *(CHR) (NONE)*

- G -

Goatesuck "Goats" (The name they gave the white man's goat). *(W)*

- H -

Hannoo One of the Indian Jurors at the trial of the murderers of John Sassamon. *(PCR)*

Hassanamesit "The place of small stones", now Grafton, Massachusetts. *(E) (G) (MHC)*

Hassaneghk Word used to describe unusual stone-sided dwelling of an early settler at Westport, Massachusetts. It is interesting to note how the English has through the years corrupted it into the word "Horseneck" Beach, Massachusetts. "Hassa" meaning stones, and "Neghk" describing the "Peaked" roof. *(E) (G) (W) (OTR) (H-B) (ALLEN HIST.)*

Hawkswawney "The time of leisure and story telling". Actually this word describes the lazy flight of the birds of prey, and of the Indian's mood and dreams of being able to fly and hunt in such a manner. *(ALLEN HIST.) (N.B. PUBLIC LIBRARY)*

Hiacoomes Disciple of the Mayhews and first christian Wampanoag on Martha's Vineyard, Massachusetts. *(M) (G)*

Hobbomock	One of the famous warriors of the Wampanoag Indians. He was somewhat of an "Ambassador" sent by Massasoit to aid and live with the Pilgrims at Plymouth. *(PCR) (D) (MR) (PHG)*
Hobomoko	"The devil", one of their evil spirits. *(W)*
Hogsuck or Pigsuck	The name they applied to the white man's pig as distinguished from their wild pigs. *(W)*
Honck, Honckock or Wompatuck-shauog	"Goose or geese" *(W)*
Hoquanun-aunash	"Hook - hooks" (fish) *(W)*
Housantonic	"Beyond the mountains" *(NONE) (E) (G) (MAS)*
Hummanaquem	An Indian convert at Martha's Vineyard and first pastor of a congregation there. (M) (G)
Hutmoiden	An Indian Warrior leader of the Wampanoags. *(D)*
Hyannis	A mutilation of Iyanough. The name of a town in Barnstable County on Cape Cod, Massachusetts. *(PCR) (B-H) (OTR)*

- I -

Iootash	A battle word to signify "Stand Firm!" *(CHURCH)*
Iroquois	The name of the Indian Nation whose Federation included the Cayugas, Sennecas, Oneidas, Onondagos and Mohawks. *(S)*
Issack	One of the Indian guards who served at the temporary Indian prisoner camps in the area now called "Indian Neck" at Wareham, Massachusetts. *(CHURCH) (PHG)*
Iyanough	The Chief of the Mattakeeset Tribute Tribe of the Wampanoags and a Sagamore of the Federation. Hyannis & Wiano are towns on Cape Cod, Massachusetts derived from his name. *(PCR) (H-B) (OTR) (TALES OF CAPE COD, INC.)*

- J -

Juhetteke	A battle word of encouragement. *(W)*

- K -

Kanoonus	A leader of the Mashpee-Wampanoags. *(BHS)*
Katamas	Legendary Indian character of the Aquinna-Wampanoags. *(OTR) (VANDERHOOP)*
Kattenanit, Job	A praying Indian of Hassanamesit. *(E) (G)*
Kaukakineamuck or Pebenochichauquanick	"A looking glass" *(W)*
Kaukont-tuock	"Crow - crows" *(W)*
Kausitteks	"Hot weather" *(W)*
Kautantouwit	"The house of the Great South west God" from whence came all their beneficial things. *(W)*
Keduskeag	"Place of eels" now Bangor, Maine. *(NONE)*
Keegsquaw	"A maiden" *(W)*
Keehchuckquaset	"The great toe"
Keen	"Brave" *(WINSLOW) (MR) (PCR)*
Keencomsett	A sub-chief of the Mattakeeset-Wampanoags. *(PCR) (H-B)*
Keenomp, Negonshachick	"Brave warriors" *(W)*
Keesaqushin	"High tide" *(W)*
Keesqush Keesuck-Quai	"Coming by day" *(W)*
Keesuckquant	"The Sun God" *(W)*
Kehonowsquaw, Sarah	The wife of John Tahattawan, and later the wife of Oonamog. *(B-H) (E) (G)*
Kemechetteas	"To creep" *(W)*
Kennebec	A river in Maine *(OCR) (NONE)*
Kepenummin or Wuttunnemun	"To gather corn" *(W)*

Kikimuit

"The path or place where the otter passes" now the site of Swansea, Massachusetts, and one of the royal villages of the Wampanoag Federation. It is another example as to how most of the Wampanoag words have been mutilated as it was originally "Nkekemauett" with "Nkeke" meaning otter and "mau" meaning path, and "ett" meaning place. *(FESS. R.I. 13, 27, 65) (R.I.-HK-COL. I, p. 95) (W)*

Kitonuck

"The white man's ship" *(W)*

Kitsuog

"Cormorants" *(W)*

Kittaumut

Name of one of the Tribute Tribes of the Wampanoag Federation. *(H-B) (OTR) (SI)*

Krietta

"A bundle of joy" *(W) (B-H) (OTR) (PIPER)*

Kunnanaumpa-
summish

"Mercy! Mercy!" *(W)*

Kunnosnep

"To anchor or tie up the boat" *(W)*

Kuttiomp or
Paucot-tauwaw

"A great buck" *(W)*

Kuttowonck

The name given to the Englishmen's trumpet. *(W)*

- M -

Mannexit

An Indian village where now stands Woodstock. *(OCR) (E) (G)*

Machequoce

"A girdle of wampum" *(W)*

Machetu

"A poor man" *(W)* He has no wetu *(HOME)*

Machippog

"A quiver" *(W)*

Machipscat

"A stone path" *(W)*

Magunkaquoag
(Magunkook)

"Place of great trees", now Hopkinton. *(OTR)*

Manitoo

"The God" *(W)*

Mamaneway

The Indian name of Peter Awashonks, the

son of the Squaw Sachem of the Sakonnets. *(See Awashonks) (D) (RHC) (DUBUQUE)*

Manamookeagin "Place of many beaver", now Abington, Massachusetts. *(NONE) (MHC) (OTR) (H-B)*

Manamoyk
(Monomoy) The name of one of the Tribute Tribes of the Wampanoags once located on Cape Cod, Massachusetts. *(D) (H-B) (OTR) (MR) (SI)*

Manisimmin "To cut or mow" *(W)*

Manittooes or
Manit or
Manittowock "God or Gods" *(W)*

Mannochamock or
Wanackmanak The name of the Chief of one of the Tribute Tribes of the Wampanoags once located on Nantucket Island, Massachusetts. *(M) (G) (MHC) (OTR)*

Mannsu "Sober and chaste" *(W)*

Mapannog "The breast" *(W)*

Maquas The Wampanoag name for the Mohawks. *(NONE) (D)*

Masaunock "Flax" *(W)*

Mashamiapaine Chief of the Nobsuosset-Wampanoags once located on Cape Cod, Massachusetts. *(H-B) (OTR) (SI)*

Mashpee Now the accepted spelling of the Indian village located on Cape Cod, Massachusetts. Here is another excellent example of word mutilation that is traceable without doubt. Originally it came from "Mass" meaning great, "Seip" meaning a river, and "Pi" or "Pee" used as a "slur" instead of "ett" which means place. Hence, "Masseippee" (note how close this is to Mississippi) and is said to mean "A great river coming from a pond bearing many fish". Through the years this word has come down in many variations, from "Masseippee" to "Massapee" to "Mashpee". (The present Wampanoag descendants prefer to call themselves "Marshpees".) *(OTR) (MHC III:175) (W) (H-B) (MARSH-PEE INDIANS)*

Mashtuxet

"The clear water" (as in a brook or pool). *(OTR) H-B)*

Maskippague

One of the Indian jurors at the John Sassamon murder trial. *(PCR) (D) (MR) (PHG)*

Maskitauash

"Grass or hay" *(W)*

Massachusetts

"Place of the big hill", now Blue Hills, comes from "Massa" meaning big or great and "Chu" meaning hill or hills and "ett" meaning place or places. The people living within this area were of the Massachusetts Indian Federation closely allied to the Wampanoags and with them and the Pequots, Narragansetts and the Pawtuckets formed part of the Algonquian Indian Nation. *(MHC) (W) (E) (G)*

Massasoit

The Sachem of the Wampanoag Indian Federation at the time of the Pilgrims' landing. He died in the year 1661. He was the father of Wamsutta (Alexander) and Pometcom (King Philip). His tribal name was Ousamequin (yellow feather), but he later changed it to Massasoit to comply with the English counterpart, "The Great Leader" as he was called by the Pilgrims. It comes from "Massa" meaning great and "asoyt" meaning leader. *(BICKNEL'S SOWAMS) (OTR) (D) (PCR) (MR) (W) (INDIAN BIOG. I:140) (PHG)*

Maswasehi

"Where the great bird of prey lives", now called Monument Mountain and located in Great Barrington. *(OTR) (E) (MAS)*

Mataquason

The name of the chief of the Manamoyk-Wampanoags once located at Cape Cod, Massachusetts. *(H-B) (OTR) (SI)*

Matit

"An unloaded gun" *(W)*

Matoonas	A chief of the Nipmuck Tribe who was captured during King Philip's war and shot in Boston Common. *(MHC) (E) (G)*
Mattaasu	"A little way" *(W)*
Mattagehan	"A cross wind" *(W)*
Mattakeeset	The name of one of the Wampanoag Tribute Tribes once located on Cape Cod, Massachusetts. *(H-B) (OTR) (SI) (PCR) (MR)*
Mattapan	"A good place to set camp" *(NONE)*
Mattapoisett	"At the resting place". It was the name of one of the Wampanoag Tribute Tribes located in the area now called Swansea, Massachusetts. It is now the name applied by an early settler to Mattapoisett, Massachusetts. *(CHURCH'S HIST.) (DEXTER, p. 19) (OTR) (H-B)*
Mattashunannonma	One of the Indians convicted of murdering John Sassamon. *(PCR) (MR) (D) (PHG)*
Mattauqus	"A cloud" *(W)*
Matwaunonck	"A battle" *(W)*
Matwauog	"Soldiers" *(W)*
Mauchatea	"A guide" *(W)*
Mauchauhom	"A dead man" *(W)*
Mauchauhomwodk-Chepeck	"The dead" *(W)*
Maumichemanege	"A needle" *(W)*
Maunetu	"A conjurer" (God given) *(W)*
Mautamp	The name of the Sachem of Quaboag. *(MHC) (E) (G)*
Manchage	The Indian village where now stands Oxford. *(OTR)*
Mecautea	"A warrior" *(W)*
Menemsha	A pond located at Martha's Vineyard, Massachusetts. *(OTR) (NONE)*

Merrimack	"Place where there are plenty of sturgeon", now the name of the river. *(IND. WARS-SYLVESTER)*
Meteauhock	The periwinkle (conch). *(W)*
Metewis	"Black earth" *(W)*
Miacomit	One of the Wampanoag Tribute Tribes once located on Cape Cod, Massachusetts. *(H-B) (OTR) (SI)*
Miantonomo	A Sachem of the Narragansett Indian Federation. *(RHC) (D)*
Miawene	"A court, or meeting" *(W)*
Michokateh	"When it thaws" *(W)*
Micuckaskeete	"A meadow" *(W)*
Mihtuck-Quash	"Tree - trees" *(W)*
Minikesu	"Strong" *(W)*
Minioquesu	"Weak" *(W)*
Mionie	The name of Massasoit's only known daughter. *(IHG) (PCR)*
Mippauochaumen	"We are dancing" *(W)*
Mishanneke-Quock	"Squirrel - squirrels" *(W)*
Mishaum	"A place where it is windy" (windy hill). *(NONE) (W) (OTR)*
Mishaupen	"A great wind" *(W)*
Mishcup-Pauog or Sequanamau-Quock	The small salt water fish now called "scup". *(W)*
Mishimmayagat	"A great path" *(W)*
Mishitashin	"A storm" *(W)*
Mishittouwand	"A great canoe" as applied to white man's ship. *(W)*
Mishoon	The Wampanoag dugout made from a pine, oak or chestnut tree. *(W)*
Mishoonemese	"A canoe" (small dugout). *(W)*
Mishquammauquock	"Red fish" (salmon). *(W)*

Mishquashim	"A red fox" *(W)*
Mishquawtuck	"Cedar tree" *(W)*
Mishque, Neepuck	"Blood" *(W)*
Mishquinuit	"Red cloth" *(W)*
Mishquock	"Red earth" *(W)*
Misqui	"Red" *(W)*
Misqushkon	"Trout"
Missinnege	The title given to the leader of all the Wampanoag warriors. The Head Panseis. *(Viz.* Anawon*) (W) (WEEKS, MASSASOIT)*
Missittopu	"A great frost" *(W)*
Missuckeke-Kequock	"Bass" (a fish). *(W)*
Missuppaugatch	"When the rivers are open" (unfrozen). *(W)*
Mittark	A chief at Martha's Vineyard, Massachusetts. *(OTR) (PCR) (JEFFERS)*
Moamitteaug	"Frost fish" *(W)*
Moaskug	"A black snake" *(W)*
Mockuttasuit	This was the title given to a person of high esteem whose duty it was to wrap the dead body in mats and skins and prepare it for burial. *(W)*
Mocrust	An Indian leader of the Marshpee-Wampanoags. *(PCR) (OTR) (D)*
Mocussinass or Mockussinchass	"Soft leather shoes" *(W)*
Mohcont-Tash	"A foot - feet" *(W)*
Mohegan (Mohicans)	"A bewitched wolf". Name of a tribe native to the Maine area. *(CHR) (D)*
Mohewonck	"A raccoon pelt" *(W)*
Mokassuck	"Finger nails" *(W)*
Monaskunnemun	"To weed" *(W)*
Monaskunnummau- towin	"The weeding or broad hoe" *(W)*

Monequassum

An Indian school master at the "Praying Town" of Natick. *(E) (G) (OTR)*

Monoco

"One-Eyed-John" a hostile Nipmuck Chief. *(CHURCH)*

Monponsett

The name of one of the Royal Wampanoag Indian villages and the site of a Tribute Tribe of the Wampanoags. Now the area of Halifax, Massachusetts. *(B-H) (OTR) (SI) (PCR) (MR)*

Montaup

The residence of King Philip and one of the Tribute Tribes of the Wampanoags. It is a corruption of the Indian word "Uppaquantaup". It has now been mutilated to "Mount Hope" and is within the locality now Bristol, Rhode Island. *(W) (E) (OTR) (HAFF. IND. MUSEUM - RECORDS)*

Montowampate

The son of the Squaw Sachem of Wachusetts. *(MHC)*

Monyocam

The name of the Chief who was the Sagamore of the Acushnet, Apponagansett and Acoaxet Tribute Tribes of the Wampanoags that were native to the locality now Acushnet, New Bedford, Dartmouth and Westport, Massachusetts. *(OLD DART. HIST. REC.) (ROB. CAVERLEY) (DEED TO NOKATAY) (SI)*

Moonanam (Wamsutta)

One of Alexander's Indian names. Massasoit's eldest son. *(PCR) (D) (IHG)*

Moose

The name they applied to moose skin. *(W)*

Moosquin

"A moose fawn" *(W)*

Moshup

The legendary Indian giant of the Martha's Vineyard Tribes. *(VANDERHOOP) (OTR)*

Mount Hope

The present accepted corruption of "Montaup" and "Uppaquontaup". The royal residence of King Philip now located in Bristol, Rhode Island. *(W) (OTR) (See Montaup) (REC. INDIAN MUSEUM, BRISTOL)*

Mowashuck	"Iron" *(W)*
Mowi-Sucki	"Black" *(W)*
Moscattuck	"The forehead" *(W)*
Muchetan or Skat	"Low tide" *(W)*
Muchickehea	"Fruitful" *(W)*
Muckiis-Auhaqut	"A child's head dress" *(W)*
Muckquachuck-Quand	"The children's God" *(W)*
Muckquashim-Wock	"Wolf - wolves" *(W)*
Muckquetu	"Swift" *(W)*
Muckucki	"Bare cloth without wool" *(W)*
Muhhekunnuck	"At the spot where the waters are constantly in motion" (a water current). *(W) (E) (G)*
Munnote-Tash	"Basket - baskets" *(W)*
Munnucks-Munnuck Suck	"Brant - Brantgeese" *(W)*
Musketaquid	"Grassy brook", now the site of Concord, Massachusetts. *(OTR)*
Myoxeo	A Christian Indian of Martha's Vineyard, Massachusetts. *(M) (G)*
Mystic, Mystuck	A small river in Massachusetts. *(NONE)*

- N -

Nahanton	An early Christian Indian who lived at Dorchester Mill. *(E) (G)*
Namaske	"Place to Fish" located on the Merrimack River. *(NONE)*
Namaskeket	"A good place to set out for (Cod) fish", now the site of Eastham, Massachusetts on Cape Cod and the place of the famous "First Encounter" with the Pilgrims. *(OTR) (MR) (PCR)*
Namaus-suck	"Fish-many fish" *(W)*
Namquatnumack	A leader of the Marshpee-Wampanoags. *(OTR) (BHS)*

Nanaquaket	"The place of dangerous water". Comes from the word "Nunnukque" meaning dangerous. This spot is located at Tiverton near the Island of Rhode in Rhode Island. *(CHURCH'S HIST. - DEXTER,* p. *8) (D) (OTR)*
Nanepashemet	"The new moon". The name of a Sachem of the Massachusetts Indian Federation. *(MHC) (D)*
Nanepaushat	Their name for the moon and the moon god. *(W)*
Nanockquittin	"The south east wind" *(W)*
Nanouwetea	"An overseer or orderer of their worship" *(W)*
Nantasket	An Indian village now the site of Hull, Massachusetts. *(OTR) (NONE)*
Nantucket	The name of an Island off the coast of Massachusetts. (It is interesting to note that on a map dated 1630 this island was spelled Noatucke.) *(NONE)*
Naoas	The name of an early christian Indian of Hassanamesit. *(E) (G)*
Naotucke	This is believed to be the correct phonetic spelling for Nantucket, as taken down from the Indian's pronunciation. *(See Nantucket) (NONE)*
Narragansett	The name of the Indian Federation native to Rhode Island and parts of Connecticut. They and the Pawtuckets, Wampanoags, Pequots and Massachusetts formed the Algonquian Indian Nation native to the area now New England. *(RHC) (SWANTON)*
Nashaguitsa	The Indian name of a penninsula at Martha's Vineyard, Massachusetts. *(OTR) (NONE)*
Nashamoiess	The name of one of the Wampanoag Tribute Tribes once located on Cape Cod, Massachusetts. *(B-H) (OTR) (SI)*

Nashanekammuck	The name of one of the Wampanoag Tribute Tribes once located on Cape Cod, Massachusetts. *(B-H) (OTR) (SI)*
Nashaways or Hashuas	The Indian tribe native to New Hampshire in the Lancaster area. *(SWANTON)*
Nashobah	Now the site of Littleton. *(E) (NONE) (D)*
Naskeag	"Good places for shell fishing" *(NONE)*
Nataous	An early christian Indian who lived at Natick. *(E) (G)*
Natick	"A place in the hills" *(E)*
Natoquashunck	"A wolf's skin" *(W)*
Natouwompitea	"One who makes the wampum" *(W)*
Naukocks nonkan-nawi	"Coming by night" *(W)*
Naummatin or Sunnadin	"The north wind" *(W)*
Naumpacouin	"To hang about the neck" (necklace) *(W)*
Naushon	The name of one of the small Elizabethan Islands. *(NONE)*
Nawwatick	"Far out at sea" *(W)*
Nawwauqaquaw	"Afternoon" *(W)*
Naynayyoumewot	The name they applied to the Englishman's "horse" as they had no horses of their own prior to the coming of the English. *(W)*
Neechipog	"The dew" *(W)*
Neeshauog or Sassamuaquock or Nquitteconnauog	"Eels" *(W)*
Nees quittow	"A long house with two fires" *(W)*
Negonschick, Keenomp	"Brave warriors" *(W)*
Neimpauog	"Thunder" *(W)*
Neimpauog pesk homwock	"Thunderbolts" *(W)*

Nemasket	"At the fishing place". The name of one of the Tribute Tribes of the Wampanoags. Now the site of Middleboro, Massachusetts. *(OTR) (PCR) (MR) (DEXTER, p. 31) (SI)*
Nesutan, Job	An Indian interpreter that worked with the Rev. John Elliot. *(E)*
Netasuog	The name the Wampanoags gave to the white man's "cattle" *(W)*
Netop-pauog	"Friend - friends" *(W) (PCR)*
Neyhome-mauog	"Turkey - turkeys" *(W)*
Neyhommauashunck	"The turkey head dress" *(W)*
Nickanoose	A chief of one of the Nantucket Tribute Tribes of the Wampanoags. *(B-H) (D) (MR) (OTR) (M)*
Nickautick	A kind of "wooden pincers or vice" *(W)*
Nickommo	"A feast or dance" *(W)*
Nickommosach- miawene	"The council and feast ordered by the great Sachem" *(W)*
Nipmuck	"The fresh water people". The name of a tribe of Indians native to the area now New Hampshire and Vermont and Worcester County. *(D) (W) (DEXTER, p. 17)*
Nippawus	"The sun" *(W)*
Nip	Drinking water (to drink) - spring water
Nips	"Pond" *(W)*
Nipsach	"Ponds" *(W)*
Nishohkou	An early christian Indian who lived at Natick. *(E)*
Niss-nissoke	"Kill! Kill!" *(W)*
Nittauke Nissa- wanawkamuck	"My land" (this is my land) *(W)*
Nkeke Nkequock	"Otter - otters" *(W)*
Nkequashunck	"The otter's pelt" *(W)*
Nnappaqnat	"Dry weather" *(W)*

Nnapi	"Dry" *(W)*
Nobsuosset	The name of one of the Wampanoag Tribute Tribes once located on Cape Cod, Massachusetts. *(H-B) (OTR) (SI)*
Nohtoakfact	A chief of one of the Wampanoag Tribute Tribes once located on Martha's Vineyard. *(M) (OTR)*
Nokatay	The name of a small Indian Village once located near the source of the Acushnet River now the site of New Bedford, Massachusetts. *(HIST. - COOK) (OTR)*
Nonquit (Nonquid)	The Indian name of a cove located near Tiverton, Rhode Island. This name was later given to an area in So. Dartmouth, Massachusetts by a settler from Rhode Island. *(NARRATIVE, 97) (BRIEF HISTORY, 39) (OTR)*
Noosup or Sumhup-pauog	"Beaver or beavers" *(W)*
Nop	Salt Water (undrinkable)
Nopatin	"The East wind" *(W)*
Nope	The Indian name applied to the whole area of Martha's Vineyard, Massachusetts. *(M) (OTR)*
Nosenemuck	"Son-in-law" *(W)*
Nonantum	"A place of happiness or rejoicing". The christian Indian town established by Rev. John Eliot. It is now the site of Newton, Massachusetts. *(E)*
Npeshwaog	"Wild fowl", the name applied to all wild fowl. *(W)*
Ntakesemin	"Counting" *(W)*
Numpas	One of the Indian guards assigned to the Indian prisoner compound once located at Indian Neck in Wareham, Massachusetts. *(PCR V 215)*
Numphow	An Indian leader of the converts at Wamesit. *(E)*

Numpouce	A son of Awashonks. *(See Awashonks)*.
Nunpaug	One of the Wampanoag Tribute Tribes located at Martha's Vineyard, Massachusetts. *(B-H) (OTR) (SI)*

- O -

Obbatinnua	One of the warrior leaders of the Wampanoags. *(PCR) (D)*
Occapeeches	"Little strong drinks" (liquor). It is a diminutive from "Occape" or "Onkuppe" meaning strong drink. *(E) (DEXTER, p. 24)*
Ockqutchanng	"A wild beast of reddish hair about the size of a pig with the same habits of a pig. From whence they gave this name to all white man's swine." *(W)*
Ohbee	"Earth"
Ohkonkemme	One of the Wampanoag Tribute Tribes that was located on Cape Cod, Massachusetts. *(B-H) (OTR) (SI)*
Okommakamesit	The name of an Indian settlement once located in the vicinity of Marlborough. *(E) (MCR)*
Omphohhannut	The name of one of the Gay Head Chiefs at Martha's Vineyard, Massachusetts. *(M) (G)*
Onawangonnakaun	"Fish bait" *(W)*
Oneko	A son of Uncas, the Mohegan Sachem. *(CHR) (D)*
Oonamog	An Indian leader at Okommakamesit. *(E)*
Ope	One of the Indian jurors at the John Sassamon murder trial. *(PCR) (MR) (PHG)*
Opponenauhock	"Oysters" *(W)*
Osacontuck	"A fat sweet fish" (haddock) *(W)*
Osomehew	A son of Awashonks. *(See Awashonks)*
Otan-nash	"Village - villages" *(W)*
Ottawas	Indians of Canada. *(SWANTON)*

Ousamequin	"Yellow Feather". One of the tribal names of Massasoit. It comes from the words "ousa" meaning yellow, and "mequin" meaning feather. *(See Massasoit) (PCR) (MR) (PHG)*

- P -

Pacusttchest	A son of Awashonks. *(See Awashonks)*
Pakachoog	The original name of the site now Worcester. *(E) (MHC)*
Pakemit	Another name for Punkapoag. It was at the site of Punkapoag (spring in red earth) that a group of Indian converts established a Christian Indian Town called Pakemit. *(E) (G)*
Pamontaquash	"The Pond Sachem". He was believed to be the father of Tuspaquin. *(DEXTER,* p. 32*)*
Panseis	The name applied to Wampanoag warrior leaders. *(BHS) (WEEKS, MASSASOIT)*
Paomet	The name of one of the Wampanoag Tribute Tribes that was once located on Cape Cod, Massachusetts. Now Provincetown and Wellfleet. *(BHS) (OTR)*
Pakeponesso	The name of a chief of the Chappaquiddicks, one of the Wampanoag Tribute Tribes that was located on Martha's Vineyard, Massachusetts. *(E) (M) (G)*
Papone	"Winter" *(W)*
Paponetin	"The west wind" *(W)*
Paspisha	"It is sunrise" *(W)*
Pasque	The name of an Island of the Elizabethan group. *(NONE)*
Passaconaway	A great leader of the Pawtucket Indian Federation.
Passamoquoddy	"Great Pollock Waters" *(IND. WARS-SYLVESTER) (NONE)*

Pasuckuakoho-Wauog	The name applied to their football game. "Playing football" *(W)*
Pattaquonk	The name given to their steam bath huts. *(W)*
Patuxet	The name of one of the Wampanoag Tribute Tribes once located at the site now Plymouth, Massachusetts. *(MR) (PCR)*
Patuxette	"Place of small falls" *(NONE) (OTR)*
Pauchautaqua-Nesash	"Branch - branches" *(W)*
Pauganaut, Tamwock	"Cod fish" *(W)*
Paugautemisk	"An oak tree" *(W)*
Pauguautemis-saund	"An oak canoe" *(W)*
Paukunnawwaw or Mosk	"Bear" *(W)*
Paukunnum	"Dark" *(W)*
Paumpagussit	"The Sea God" *(W)*
Pauochautowwins	"A bauble" *(W)*
Paupock-suog	"Partridge - partridges" *(W)*
Paushesui	"The half moon" *(W)*
Pausinnummin	"To dry the corn" *(W)*
Pauskeseu	"Naked" *(W)*
Paweshaquaw	"Noon time" *(W)*
Pawpoesit	One of the Wampanoag Tribute Tribes once located on Cape Cod, Massachusetts. *(SI) (OTR) (H-B)*
Pawtucket	"At the place of the falls". The name of the Indian Federation that lived in the vicinity of the Merrimack. They and the Wampanoags, the Narragansetts, the Pequots, and the Massachusetts Federations formed the Algonquian Indian Nation native to New England. *(NONE) (SI)*

Peemayagat	"A little way" *(W)*
Pegan	A Natick Indian convert. *(E)*
Penashimwock	"Animals" or "Beasts". *(W)*
Penikese	"Unused sleeping land away out in the water". The name of a small island of the Elizabethan group. *(NONE)*
Pennahannit	The Indian "Marshall-general" of all the Christian Indian towns established by Eliot and Gookin. *(E) (G)*
Pennakooks	The Indians who lived in the area now Concord, New Hampshire. *(SWANTON) (SI)*
Pequawus	"A gray fox". (The black or silver fox they refused to kill and called them Manittooes, that is, Gods or Spirits or Divine Powers as they said of everything which they could not comprehend.)
Pequots or Pequod	"The gray foxes". The name of the Federated Tribes who lived in sections now parts of Connecticut. They belonged to the Algonquian Indian Nation. Some sources also list the meaning of the name as "the destroyers or enemies". In this last, it is said to root from the word "Paquatoog" which means "they destroy". *(D) (E) (W) (WINTHROP JOURNAL I 52, 72, 122)*
Peshaui	"Blue" *(W)*
Peshauiuash	"Violet leaves" *(W)*
Peskcunck	"The white man's gun" *(W)*
Petacaus	"An English waistcoat" *(W)*
Petascunnemun	"To hill the corn" *(W)*
Petononowit or Peter Nunuit	A husband of Weetammo, and an ally of the English during King Philip's war. *(PHG) (DEXTER) (OTR)*
Petunk	"That into which something is put". The pocket apron worn by male Indians. *(DEXTER) (W)*

Piambouhou   An Indian convert who lived at Nonantum.
                      (E)

Pigsguesset   The Indian name of a site now Watertown.
                      (NONE)

Pocasset   A Tribute Tribe of the Wampanoags once
                      located in the area now Fall River, Massa-
                      chusetts and Tiverton, Rhode Island. *(OTR)*
                      (PHG) (PCR) (SI)

Pohunna   The Chief of the Sakonesset-Wampanoags
                      once located in the Cape Cod area. *(B-H)*
                      (OTR) (PCR)

Pokanoket   "Place of the bitter water bays and coves".
                      The name of the Wampanoag land area.
                      (BURTON) (OTR) (H-B)

Pometacom or   "The killer of wolves". These are variations
Metacomet or   in the phonetic spelling of the tribal name
Pometacomet   of King Philip, with Pometacom being the
                      most popular spelling. *(PHG) (D) (OTR)*

Ponampum and   The names of two Indian converts who lived
Poquanum   at Natick. *(E) (G)*

Popowuttahig   "Drums". The name applied to the English-
                      man's drums as they had no drums until the
                      coming of the white man. *(W) (RHC I 38-
                      149)*

Poppakaunnetch,
Auchaugotch   "Dark night" *(W)*

Poppasquash   "Land where the partridge abounds". It
                      comes from the word "Paupocl" which
                      means partridge. It is the name given to a
                      neck of land that projects from the western
                      side of Bristol, Rhode Island. *(E) (W) (DEX-
                      TER,* p. 46*)*

Posakunnamun   "To bury" *(W)*

Posotoquo   A son of Awashonks *(See Awashonks)*

Potomska   The area now Potomska, South Dartmouth,
                      Massachusetts *(NONE)*

Potop-Pauog   "Whale, whales" *(W)*

Pottowattomies	Indians native to the Lake Michigan area. *(SWANTON)*
Pow Wow	The name of the Wampanoag medicine man. *(W) (E) (G)*
Puckhommin	"To beat or thrash out corn" *(W)*
Pumham	The name of a Narragansett chief. *(D) (RHC)*
Pumm-Pummoke	"To shoot" *(W)*
Pumpasa or Nimrod	A Wampanoag warrior leader. *(PCR) (D) (PHG)*
Pumpom	"A tribute deer skin". (When a deer is killed in the water it automatically belonged to the great sachem of the tribes and the skin was always offered to him.) *(W)*
Punckquaneck	The name of a Wampanoag warrior leader. *(PCR) (D)*
Punkatese	An Indian name applied to an area now part of Little Compton, Rhode Island. *(DEXTER, p. 31)*
Punkapoag	"A spring that rises out of red earth". Now the site of Stoughton, Massachusetts. *(E) (G) (OTR)*
Punonakauit	The Indian name of the section now Wellfleet, Massachusetts. *(OTR)*
Puppuckshackhege	"A box-like receptacle" *(W)*
Pussough	"The wild cat" *(W)*
Puttuckquapuonck	"The playing arbor". (Amusement center where games were played)

- Q -

Quabaquid or Quaboag	Now the site of Brookfield. *(MHC) (OTR) (E)*
Quachatasset	The name of the chief of the Manomet-Wampanoags. *(D) (B-H) (OTR) (PCR)*
Quadaquina	A brother of Massasoit. *(MR) (PCR)*
Quahog	"Dark colored shell". This is a mutilation

of the word "suckauhock". It actually is the name of the dark purple piece of the quahog shell from which their dark beads of wampum (money) was ground. *(W)*

Quanapohit, Thomas and James
Two "praying" Indian converts. *(E) (M)*

Quannauqussu
"A tall man" *(W)*

Quantisset
Now the site of Woodstock. *(E) (NONE)*

Quaquaquaansuke
The name of the chief of the Paomet-Wampanoags. *(OTR) (PCR)*

Quary, Abram
Believed to have been the last of the full-blooded Wampanoags who lived on Nantucket Island. He died in 1885. *(OTR)*

Quebec
"At a place that narrows". Now the name of a province in Canada. *(IND. WARS-SYLVESTER)*

Quequechan
"The place of the violent, falling waters." Now within the area of Fall River, Massachusetts at the outlet of Watuppa Pond. It comes from the phonetic sound of "chekee or Cheche" meaning violent, forcible or falling, and the "chan" here is a slur or mutilation of "ett" meaning place. *(FOWLER'S HIST. OF FALL RIVER, 27) (DEXTER, p. 12)*

Quequecum-Mauog
"Ducks" *(W)*

Quequequananachet
A Narragansett Indian and one of the husbands of Weetammo. *(PHG) (D) (RHC)*

Quinapen
A Narragansett chief. *(D) (RHC)*

Quisset or Cooxisset
The name of one of the Wampanoag Tribute Tribes once located on Cape Cod, Massachusetts. *(B-H) (OTR) (SI)*

Quittaub
A Wampanoag Tribute Tribe once located on Cape Cod, Massachusetts. *(B-H) (OTR) (SI)*

Death of King Philip at Mount Hope
(now Rhode Island), August, 1676.

Qunnekamuck	This was the name of a special long house wherein they held a special dance at harvest time. At this dance one would take the center and dance alone heavily burdened with possessions that were given away one at a time to a person who called out "Cowequetummous", that is, "I beg of you". As each dancer disposed of his belongings another would enter, and then another, and so on and on would they dance sometimes into the early hours of daybreak. *(W) (WILLIAM WOOD)*
Qunnequawese	"A very young doe" *(W)*
Qunosuog	"Fresh water fish" *(W)*
Qussuck-Anash	"Very small stones" *(W)*
Qussuckomineanug	"The cherry tree" *(W)*
Qussuk	"Rock"
Quttuck	"The throat" *(W)*

- S -

Sabbatubkett	The name of a Nobsuosset Indian. *(PHG) (PCR)*
Sachem	"The leading chief of the Federation". The word actually means "The strong one". They also applied this name to a little bird about the size of a swallow due to its "Sachem or princelike" courage and command over greater birds. They delighted in seeing this small bird pursue and frighten off the crow and other larger birds. *(W)*
Sachimmaacommock	"The name applied to the Sachem's house" *(W)*
Sachimoachwpewessin	"A strong north east wind" *(W)*
Sagamore	The name applied to chiefs who ruled more than one of the Wampanoag Tribute Tribes. All Sagamores were Panseis of the Federation. *(RB) (PCR) (PHG)*

Sakonesset
One of the Wampanoag Tribute Tribes that was located on Cape Cod, Massachusetts. *(B-H) (OTR) (SI)*

Sakonnet
"The third conquered territory". The name of the Wampanoag Tribute Tribe who lived in the area now Little Compton, Rhode Island. *(ELIOT GEN XXIV 62) (John XV 19) (DEXTER - footnote 6) (SI)*

Samoset
The first Indian to appear before the Pilgrims at Plymouth. He was a friend of Massasoit and a Sagamore of the Indians from the territory now the site of Kennebec in Maine. *(PCR) (MR) (PHG)*

Sanballet
Alias "Sam Barrow" the chief of the Agwam-Wampanoags. *(PCR V 206) (CHURCH)*

Sancheacantacket
The name of one of the Wampanoag Tribute Tribes once located on Cape Cod, Massachusetts. *(H-B) (OTR) (SI)*

Sasaunckapamuck
"The sassafras tree" *(W)*

Sassamon
Alias John Sassamon. One of the disciples of the Rev. John Eliot who helped prepare the Indian Bible. He was born in the vicinity that is now Dorchester. He was later the Indian secretary to King Philip and just prior to the outbreak of the war his body was found beneath the ice of Assawompsett Pond. His murderers were tried and convicted in a trial that assumed the proportions of the biggest event in Plymouth up to the times. It has been said that his murder was the spark that ignited the bloody King Philip War. *(E) (MR) (PHG) (MCR)*

Satuit
The name of one of the Wampanoag Tribute Tribes that was once located on Cape Cod, Massachusetts. *(H-B) (OTR) (SI)*

Saugus
Now the site of Lynn, Massachusetts *(NONE)*

Saunks
The title given to the Sachem's wife. *(W)*

Sauop	"Tomorrow" *(W)*
Saupuck	"Gun powder" *(W)*
Scannemeneash	"Seed corn" *(W)*
Schoodic	"Burnt lands". Now the name of Lake Schoodic. *(SYLVESTER)*
Sconticut	The name of one of the Wampanoag Tribute Tribes once located in the section now Fairhaven, Massachusetts. It is the present accepted spelling of the original sound, "Seconchqut". *(HIST. COOK) (OTR) (SI)*
Seekonk	The Indian definition of this word is often confused with Sakonnet. It was the name applied to the area now Seekonk, Massachusetts and is a mutilation of the word "Suckikonket" with "Sucki" meaning black and "konk" a contraction of the word for geese . . .hence, "Where the black geese abound". *(W)*
Segauo	"A widower" *(W)*
Seip	"River" *(W)*
Seip taquatsha	"The river is frozen" *(W)*
Sepakehig	"A sail" *(W)*
Sepoese	"A little river" *(W)*
Sequan	"Spring" *(W)*
Sequnnock or Popquauhock	Another name for the Quahog. (As to size). *(W)*
Sequosquaw	"A widow" *(W)*
Sequt	"The black soot with which they covered their face during periods of mourning" *(W)*
Sesek	"A rattlesnake" *(W)*
Shawanon or Sholan	"A friendly Sachem of the Nashaways" *(NONE)*
Shawmut	The name of a Tribute Tribe of the Massachusetts Indian Federation. *(OTR) (H-B) (SI)*

(From an old print in the author's collection)

SAMOSET GREETS THE PILGRIMS

The Sagamore of tribes located in the area that is now Maine. He was the first Indian to visit the Pilgrims. He was sent to Plymouth on request of Massasoit.

Shawomet	The name of one of the Wampanoag Tribute Tribes once located in the area now Falmouth, Massachusetts. *(OTR) (SI)*
Shimmoah	"A spring of special interest for quality of its water". The name of one of the Tribute Tribes of the Wampanoags once located on Cape Cod, Massachusetts. *(D) (OTR) (SI)*
Shoshanim	Alias "Sagamore Sam", a Nipmuck Chief. *(NONE)*
Siasconset	"A place near the open sea". The name of one of the Wampanoag Tribute Tribes once located on Nantucket Island, Massachusetts. *(NONE) (OTR) (SI)*
Sickissoug	"Clams" *(W)*
Sippican	"The unclear or muddy river". The name of one of the Wampanoag Tribute Tribes that was located in the area now Marion and Mattapoisett, Massachusetts. *(DEXTER, p. 28) (OTR) (H-B)*
Sitchipuck	"The neck" *(W)*
Skatekook	"At the junction of two bodies of water" *(W)*
Sochepo or Cone	"Snow" *(W)*
Sokenug	"A heap of corn" *(W)*
Sokenun	"Rain" *(W)*
Sowahagens	The name applied to the Indians north of the Nashaways. *(NONE) (SWANTON)*
Sowams	The Royal village of Massasoit that is now the site of Warren, Rhode Island. *(PCR) (OTR) (MR) (SI)*
Sowamset	"The place where the Royal village is located" *(W)*
Sowwanand	"The God that always came with the southern wind" *(W)*
Sowwanishen	"The southwest" (the direction from whence came all that was beneficial to them and the

wind that they worshipped as it brought them their most beloved God and their best weather). *(W)*

Squannakonk	"A good water fowling place" *(W)*
Squanto or Suantum or Tisquantum	The sole survivor of the Patuxet-Wampanoags at the time of the landing of the Pilgrims. He was introduced to them by Samoset and became an invaluable aid to the settlers during their first two years at Plymouth. *(PCR) (MR) (MHC) (PHG)*
Squashim	"A female" as applied to animals. *(W)*
Squauanit	"The woman's God" *(W)*
Squaus-auhaqut	"A squaw's head dress" *(W)*
Squaw sachem	"The title given to a female Indian chief" *(W)*
Squibnocket	The name of one of the peninsulas on Martha's Vineyard, Massachusetts. *(NONE)*
Succanowassuck	The name of a Rebel Sakonnet Indian. *(RHC) (DEXTER)*
Sucki	"Black" *(W)*
Suckauhock	The name given to the black part of the quahog shell and the portion from which they ground their black wampum (the most precious of their money). *(W)*
Suckinuit	"Black or blackish in color" *(W)*
Suck-ta-shompau-gatash	"A measure equivalent to a fathom in length" *(W)*
Sukkissuog-Quahog	"Clams"
Sunconwhew	The youngest son of Massasoit. *(PHG) (PCR)*
Sunnuckhig	"A falling trap made with weight of stones" *(W)*

- T -

Tabadacason	The name of the chief of the Assonet-Wampanoags. *(OTR)*

Tackanash	The name of an Indian preacher at Martha's Vineyard, Massachusetts. *(M) (G)*
Tackquiuwock	"Twins" *(W)*
Taguatchuwash	"To go up hill" *(W)*
Tahkees	"Cold" *(W)*
Tahki or Tatakki	"Cold weather" *(W)*
Takanumma	The name of one of the warrior leaders who appeared at the court at Plymouth with King Philip, Nov. 3, 1671. *(PCR)*
Takawombait	The name of Indian preacher who lived at Natick. *(E)*
Takekum	"A cold spring" (drinking water) *(W)*
Takemmy	The name of one of the Wampanoag Tribute Tribes once located on Martha's Vineyard, Massachusetts. *(OTR) (H-B) (SI)*
Talhanio	The name of one of the Wampanoag Tribute Tribes once located on Cape Cod, Massachusetts. *(OTR) (H-B) (SI)*
Taquattin	"Frost" *(W)*
Tarratines	The name of a dreaded tribe of Indians who lived in the vicinity that is now Maine and believed to be Penobscots, who once raided the Wampanoag country. *(D) (NONE) (MAS)*
Tasunsuaw	The wife of Waban. *(E)*
Taswot, John Quason	The name of the Chief of the Manamoyk-Wampanoags. *(H-B) (OTR) (D)*
Tatackommauog	"Porpoise" *(W)*
Tatatanum	One of Weetammo's names. *(W)*
Tatoson or Tautozen	This was the son of Sanballet. It was Tatoson's child who died and was buried within the swamp area of the Agawam country (see pages 144-145, *The Wampanoag Indian Federation*). This name, Tatoson, offers us an excellent opportunity to show again how careless pronounciations have caused corruptions to Indian words whereby the origi-

nal takes on a completely different spelling but traces of the sound remains. (See also Hassaneghk and Mount Hope.) Through the centuries the word Tatoson now remains as "Towser", the name of a swamp in the Rochester-Mattapoisett area. This swamp is in the territory once the lands of the Aga-wam-Wampanoags. During the King Philip War, Capt. Benjamin Church penetrated this swamp and there killed Sanballet, the Chief of the Agawams. The name of the swamp takes root in this early action and to the fact Tatoson's child was buried somewhere within the area by his mother who mysteriously fell ill and died rather than point out her child's grave as she was ordered to do by the Plymouth authorities. The settlers from then on referred to the swamp as "Tatoson's Swamp". Then through the centuries it has now assumed the sound and name, "Towser's Swamp". *(PLY COL. V 72, 205, 206, 209) (CHURCH) (OTR) (H-B) (PHG)*

Taunek-Kauog	"Crane - cranes" *(W)*
Teewaleema	The Indian name of Miss Zerviah Gould Mitchell who was a direct descendant of Massasoit in the tenth generation. She died in Lakeville, Massachusetts in 1928. *(PHG)*
Tequanomin	A pow wow who once lived at Martha's Vineyard, Massachusetts. *(M)*
Tiaquonqussichick	"Men of low statue" *(W)*
Timequassin	"To cut off or behead" *(W)*
Tisquantum	A name of Squanto *(PCR)*
Titicut	Now the Taunton River. Comes from the words "Seip-teih-tuk-qut" and meaning "the long waterway used by all". (Note also Connecticut, a corruption also; from "Con" meaning long or very long and "Titicut" meaning "the water used by all". Hence, Connecticut is meant to convey "A very long

waterway used by all the Indians".) *(ELIOT GEN. XV: 18) (CHR) (W)*

Toikiming
The name of one of the Wampanoag Tribute Tribes once located on Cape Cod, Massachusetts. *(H-B) (OTR) (SI)*

Tolony
The husband of Awashonks. (*See A-washonks.*)

Totherswamp
The name of one of the Christian Indians who lived at Natick. *(E)*

Touwuttin
"The south wind" *(W)*

Tou Wuttuttan
"What time of day is it" (actually, "how high is the sun"). *(W)*

Towanquatic
The name of one of the Indian chiefs who lived at Martha's Vineyard, Massachusetts. *(M) (G)*

Towiu-Owock
"Orphans" *(W)*

Toyusk
"A bridge" *(W)*

Tukapewillin
"A native Indian preacher at Hassanemesit" *(E)*

Tummockqua-shunck
"A beaver's pelt" *(W)*

Tummock-quoag
"Black wolf - black wolves" *(W)*

Tuppaco, Otrema-tippocat
"Towards night" *(W)*

Tuspaquin
The chief of the Assawompsett-Wampanoags and a Sagamore of the Federation. *(PHG) (PCR) (MR)*

Tutteputch
"The art of smoothing the shells on stone" (grinding out their wampum). *(W)*

- U -

Uncas
The renegade Sagamore of the Mohegans. *(CHR)*

Uppakumineash
"The seed of their squash" *(W)*

Uppaquontup
"The head" or "At the head or summit"... finally corrupted to Montaup, then Mount

Hope. It is now within the site of Bristol, Rhode Island. It was one of the Royal Villages of the Wampanoag Indian Federation and the home of King Philip. *(See Mount Hope, Montaup) (INDIAN MUSEUM, BRISTOL, R. I.) (W)*

Uppusquan   "The back" *(W)*

- W -

Waban   "The wind". A Massachusett's Indian Chief who was the Rev. John Eliot's first convert. *(E) (MHC)*

Wabquisset   An Indian village that was in the area now Woodstock. *(E)*

Wachimuqut   The name of a Wampanoag Tribute Tribe once located on Cape Cod, Massachusetts. *(OTR) H-B) (SI)*

Wachusetts   "The place about the mountain" *(DEXTER, p. 19)*

Wakoquit   One of the Wampanoag Tribute Tribes once located on Cape Cod, Massachusetts. *(OTR) (H-B) (SI)*

Wamesit   The name given to the Christian Indian Town that is now Lowell, Massachusetts. *(E) (G)*

Wampanoags   "The coastal or Eastern People" (nearly the same meaning as "Abenake"). It is the name applied to the 30 or more Federated tribes ruled by Massasoit at the time of the arrival of the Pilgrims. The Wampanoags lived in the area now parts of Rhode Island and Southeastern Massachusetts, including the Islands of Nantucket and Martha's Vineyard and also Cape Cod, Massachusetts. *(HIST. OF WAMP.) (SWANTON)*

Wampapaqum   One of the convicted murderers of John Sassamon. *(PCR)*

Wampas   The name of an Indian convert who lived at Nonantum which is now Newton, Massachusetts. *(E)*

Wampatuck   A son of Chickatabut and chief of the area which is now the site of Braintree. *(E)*

Wampum   The Indian beads made from the shell of the quahog that was used as currency. (It was their so-called white money) *(W)*

Wampumpeag   Plural for wampum (strung beads). *(W)*

Wampye (George)   One of the Indian jurors at the murder trial of John Sassamon. *(PCR)*

Wamsu   "Down hill" *(W)*

Wamsutta   Massasoit's oldest son. The name is said to mean "A loving heart" and comes from the word "Waumausu" which means loving and "wuttah" which means heart. (Waumausuttah) *(PGH) (W)*

Washuanks   A God of the Martha's Vineyard Indians. *(M)* *(VANDERHOOP)*

Wasappi   "Thin cloth" *(W)*

Wattap   "Tree root"

Wattascompanum   A sachem of the Nipmuck Indians. *(NONE)*

Watuppa   The name of one of the Indian Reservations once located in the vicinity of the present Watuppa Pond in Fall River, Massachusetts. *(DUBUQUE, HIST) (OTR)*

Wauchaunat   "A guardian" *(W)*

Waumausu   "Loving" *(W)*

Wauontakick   "Wise men" *(W)*

Wauontam   "A wise man or counselor" *(W)*

Waupi or Waban   "The wind" *(W)*

Wautaconaoug   "Coat men" which was one of their names for the white man. *(W)*

Wautacone   "A person wearing clothing", another name for the white man. *(W)*

Wautaconemese   "An English youth" *(W)*

Wautaconisk   "An English woman" *(W)*

Wauwunnegachick "Very good" *(W)*

Wanackmamak	The name of one of the Nantucket Chiefs. *(NONE) (M)*
Wawayontat or Wiwiantic	Name of one of the Wampanoag Tribute Tribes once located on Cape Cod, Massachusetts. *(H-B) (OTR) (SI)*
Wawoonettshunke	A Nobsuosset Indian. *(NONE) (D)*
Wawwhunneskesuog	"Mackrell" (fish) *(W)*
Wawwunnes	"A young buck" *(W)*
Wayaawi	"Sunset" or "The sun is down" *(W)*
Webcowet	A famous pow wow of the Massachusetts Indian Federation. *(E)*
Wechekum	"The sea" *(W)*
Weegrammomenet	"Thomas Waban", the son of Waban. *(E)*
Week, Tamson	A Gay Head Indian. *(OTR)*
Weenat	"The tongue" *(W)*
Weesquob	The name of one of the Wampanoag Tribute Tribes once located on Cape Cod, Massachusetts. *(OTR) (H-B) (SI)*
Weetammo	The daughter of Corbitant and wife of Alexander (Wamsutta). The Squaw Sachem of the Pocasset-Wampanoags and once the Saunks of the Wampanoag Indian Federation. *(PHG) (PCR) (D)*
Wekinash-quash	"Reed - reeds" *(W)*
Wekineauquat	"Fair weather" *(W)*
Wenomeneash	"Grape or grapes" *(W)*
Wepit-teash	"Tooth - teeth" *(W)*
Wequai	"Light" *(W)*
Wequash	"A swan". The name of a Christian Pequot Indian. *(E)*
Wequashim	"Moon light" *(W)*
Wesassu	"Afraid" *(W)*
Wesaui or Ousa	"Yellow" *(W)*
Wesheck	"Hair" *(W)*

Wesquaubenan	"To wrap up the dead body in mats and skins" *(W)*
Weta	"The woods" *(W)*
Wetompachick	"Comrades" *(W)*
Wetu	The name applied to a small one family home. *(W)*
Wetuomanit	"The god of their homes" *(W)*
Wewayewitt or Tolony	Another Indian name for the husband of Awashonks. *(See Awashonks)*
Wianno	A contraction of Hyannis and a mutilation of Iyanough. Now the name of a small hamlet on Cape Cod, Massachusetts. *(OTR)(HB) (TALES OF CAPE COD, INC.)*
Wickaboag	A pond in Brookfield. *(E)*
Winnepurket	A chief of the Massachusetts Indian Federation. *(E)*
Wnahtukook	"The exact spot where a spring bubbles from the earth" *(E)(W)*
Wompanand	"The Eastern God that came with the East wind" *(W)*
Wompequayi	"Any cloth with a color just off white" *(W)*
Wompesu	"White" (tending toward white in color). *(W)*
Wompi	"White" *(W)*
Wompimineash	"Chestnuts" *(W)*
Wompimish	"A chestnut tree" *(W)*
Wompimissaund	"A canoe made from the chestnut tree" (dugout). *(W)*
Wompinuit	"White cloth" *(W)*
Wompiscannemeneash	"White seed corn" *(W)*
Wompissacuk-quauog	"The eagle - eagles" *(W)*
Wonohaquaham	"Sagamore John", the son of Nanepashamet. *(E)*
Wootonanuske	The wife of King Philip and a sister of Weetammo. One of the Saunks of the Wampanoag Indian Federation. *(PHG)*

Wuchaun	"The nose" *(W)*
Wuchipoquame-neash	"Beach plum" *(W)*
Wuhock	"The body" *(W)*
Wunnaks	"The stomac" *(W)*
Wunnanameanit	"The God of the Northern Winds" *(W)*
Wunnauanounuck	The name applied to the white man's Shallop. *(W)*
Wunnauanounuck-quese	The name applied to "a skiff". *(W)*
Wunnaugon-hommin	"Their game of plumbstones" *(W)*
Wunnegehan or Wunnegin Waupi	"Fair wind" *(W)*
Wunnepog-quash	"Leaf - leaves" *(W)*
Wunnicheke	"The hand" *(W)*
Wunnickegannash	"The hands" *(W)*
Wuppittene-enash	"The arm or the arms" *(W)*
Wuskan	"A bone" *(W)*
Wuskapehanna	"New traps" *(W)*
Wuskaukamuck	"Newly worked ground" *(W)*
Wuskeesuck-quash	"The eye - eyes" *(W)*
Wuskene	"A young man" *(W)*
Wuskowhan	"A pigeon" *(W)*
Wuskowhanna-naukit	"Good pigeon country" *(W)*
Wuskowunan	"The hawk" which they domesticated and kept close to their gardens to frighten off marauders. *(W)*
Wussoquat	"A walnut tree" *(W)*
Wussuckqun	"A tail" *(W)*
Wusswaqua-tomineug	"Walnuts" *(W)*
Wutkunck	"A paddle or oar" *(W)*

Wuttah   "The heart" *(W)*

Wuttahimnasippa-
  quash   "Strawberry leaves" *(W)*

Wuttahimneash   "Strawberries" *(W)*

Wuttanho   "A staff" (walking stick). *(W)*

Wuttamauog   "Indian tobacco". The seed of Nicotania Rustica. The plant still grows wild in old fields, a relic of cultivation by Indians. *(SYL-VESTER-IND. WARS) (W)*

Wuttammagon or
  Hopuonck   "The tobacco pipe" *(W)*

Wuttip   "The brain" *(W)*

Wuttone   "The mouth" *(W)*

Wuttununoh-
  konkooh   "A humble or lowly woman". The name of an Indian woman who lived at Martha's Vineyard. *(OTR)*

Wuttouqog   "Ears" *(W)*

- Y -

Yo mtunnock   "The right hand" *(W)*

Yo nmunnatch   "The left hand" *(W)*

Yo ockquitteunk   "The new moon" *(W)*

Yotaanit   "The fire God" *(W)*